My Personal Travel Journal

_____

Any trip worth taking is worth writing about

This 8 x 10, 150 page book is a vacation or trip planner, personal travel journal that you write in.

It includes everything you need to plan, organize and enjoy your journey. It's the perfect way to organize your trip and record it for posterity and future generations to enjoy.

Packed with everything you need to plan your special journey it contains areas for you to write in and chronicle your journeys together.

Copyright Caprica Publishing 2019

No portion of this publication may be reproduced or transmitted in any form or by any means, electronic or mechanical, including, but not limited to, audio recordings, facsimiles, photocopying, or information storage and retrieval systems without explicit written permission from the author or publisher.

VACATION *Planner*

DATE OF TRIP: **DURATION:**

NOTES

TRAVEL *Bucket List*

PLACES I WANT TO VISIT:

THINGS I WANT TO SEE:

TOP 3 DESTINATIONS:

TRAVEL *Planner*
PRE-TRAVEL CHECKLIST

1 MONTH BEFORE

☐
☐
☐
☐
☐

2 WEEKS BEFORE

☐
☐
☐
☐
☐

1 WEEK BEFORE

☐
☐
☐
☐
☐

2 DAYS BEFORE

☐
☐
☐
☐
☐

24 HOURS BEFORE

☐
☐
☐
☐
☐

DAY OF TRAVEL

☐
☐
☐
☐
☐

VACATION *Planner*
DAILY ITINERARY

DATE:

LOCATION:

BUDGET:

TOP ACTIVITIES

MEAL PLANNER

TIME: SCHEDULE:

EXPENSES

TOTAL COST:

NOTES:

PACKING Check List

DOCUMENTS

- ☐ PASSPORT
- ☐ DRIVER'S LICENSE
- ☐ VISA
- ☐ PLANE TICKETS
- ☐ LOCAL CURRENCY
- ☐ INSURANCE CARD
- ☐ HEALTH CARD
- ☐ OTHER ID
- ☐ HOTEL INFO
- ☐ _____

CLOTHING

- ☐ SOCKS
- ☐ SWIM WEAR
- ☐ T-SHIRTS
- ☐ JEANS/PANTS
- ☐ SHORTS
- ☐ SKIRTS / DRESSES
- ☐ JACKET / COAT
- ☐ SLEEPWEAR
- ☐ SHOES
- ☐ _____

PERSONAL ITEMS

- ☐ SHAMPOO
- ☐ RAZORS
- ☐ COSMETICS
- ☐ HAIR BRUSH
- ☐ LIP BALM
- ☐ WATER BOTTLE
- ☐ SOAP
- ☐ TOOTHBRUSH
- ☐ JEWELRY
- ☐ _____

ELECTRONICS

- ☐ CELL PHONE
- ☐ CHARGER
- ☐ LAPTOP
- ☐ BATTERIES
- ☐ EARPHONES
- ☐ FLASH DRIVE
- ☐ MEMORY CARD
- ☐ _____
- ☐ _____
- ☐ _____

HEALTH & SAFETY

- ☐ HAND SANITIZER
- ☐ SUNSCREEN
- ☐ VITAMIN
- ☐ BANDAIDS
- ☐ ADVIL/TYLENOL
- ☐ GLASSES
- ☐ COLD/FLU MEDS
- ☐ _____
- ☐ _____
- ☐ _____

ESSENTIALS

- ☐ _____
- ☐ _____
- ☐ _____
- ☐ _____
- ☐ _____
- ☐ _____
- ☐ _____
- ☐ _____
- ☐ _____
- ☐ _____

FLIGHT *Information*

DATE: DESTINATION:

AIRLINE:	
BOOKING NUMBER:	
DEPARTURE DATE:	
BOARDING TIME:	
GATE NUMBER:	
SEAT NUMBER:	
FLIGHT DURATION:	
ARRIVAL / LANDING TIME:	

DATE: DESTINATION:

AIRLINE:	
BOOKING NUMBER:	
DEPARTURE DATE:	
BOARDING TIME:	
GATE NUMBER:	
SEAT NUMBER:	
FLIGHT DURATION:	
ARRIVAL / LANDING TIME:	

TRAVEL *Information*

DESTINATION: **DATE:**

PLACES TO STAY

THINGS TO SEE

WHERE TO EAT

RECOMMENDATIONS

TRIP BUDGET *Planner*

TRIP DETAILS:

AMOUNT NEEDED:

OUR GOAL DATE:

DEPOSIT TRACKER

AMOUNT DEPOSITED: **DATE DEPOSITED:**

TRAVEL *Information*

CAR RENTAL INFORMATION

COMPANY:

ADDRESS:

PHONE NUMBER:

CONFIRMATION #:

TOTAL COST:

EVENT INFORMATION

EVENT NAME:

LOCATION:

PHONE NUMBER:

START TIME:

OTHER:

NOTES

TRAVEL *Information*

HOTEL INFORMATION

NAME OF HOTEL:

ADDRESS:

PHONE NUMBER:

CONFIRMATION #:

RATE PER NIGHT:

FLIGHT INFORMATION

AIRLINE:

LOCATION:

FLIGHT #:

CHECK IN TIME:

DEPARTURE TIME:

REFERENCE #:

NOTES

TRIP TO DO *List*

PACKING *Check List*

DATE OF TRIP: **DURATION:**

OUTFIT *Planner*

DAY: **DESTINATION:** **PACKED:** ☐

DAY: **EVENING:**

ACTIVITY:
OUTFIT:
SHOES:
ACC:

DAY: **DESTINATION:** **PACKED:** ☐

DAY: **EVENING:**

ACTIVITY:
OUTFIT:
SHOES:
ACC:

DAY: **DESTINATION:** **PACKED:** ☐

DAY: **EVENING:**

ACTIVITY:
OUTFIT:
SHOES:
ACC:

OUTFIT *Planner*

DAY: **DESTINATION:** **PACKED:** ☐

        DAY: **EVENING:**

ACTIVITY:

OUTFIT:

SHOES:

ACC:

DAY: **DESTINATION:** **PACKED:** ☐

        DAY: **EVENING:**

ACTIVITY:

OUTFIT:

SHOES:

ACC:

DAY: **DESTINATION:** **PACKED:** ☐

        DAY: **EVENING:**

ACTIVITY:

OUTFIT:

SHOES:

ACC:

OUTFIT *Planner*

DAY: DESTINATION: PACKED: ☐

DAY: EVENING:

ACTIVITY:

OUTFIT:

SHOES:

ACC:

DAY: DESTINATION: PACKED: ☐

DAY: EVENING:

ACTIVITY:

OUTFIT:

SHOES:

ACC:

DAY: DESTINATION: PACKED: ☐

DAY: EVENING:

ACTIVITY:

OUTFIT:

SHOES:

ACC:

OUTFIT *Planner*

DAY: **DESTINATION:** **PACKED:** ☐

DAY: **EVENING:**

ACTIVITY:
OUTFIT:
SHOES:
ACC:

DAY: **DESTINATION:** **PACKED:** ☐

DAY: **EVENING:**

ACTIVITY:
OUTFIT:
SHOES:
ACC:

DAY: **DESTINATION:** **PACKED:** ☐

DAY: **EVENING:**

ACTIVITY:
OUTFIT:
SHOES:
ACC:

OUTFIT *Planner*

DAY: **DESTINATION:**   **PACKED:** ☐

DAY: **EVENING:**

- **ACTIVITY:**
- **OUTFIT:**
- **SHOES:**
- **ACC:**

DAY: **DESTINATION:**   **PACKED:** ☐

DAY: **EVENING:**

- **ACTIVITY:**
- **OUTFIT:**
- **SHOES:**
- **ACC:**

DAY: **DESTINATION:**   **PACKED:** ☐

DAY: **EVENING:**

- **ACTIVITY:**
- **OUTFIT:**
- **SHOES:**
- **ACC:**

OUTFIT *Planner*

DAY: DESTINATION: PACKED: ☐

DAY: EVENING:

ACTIVITY:

OUTFIT:

SHOES:

ACC:

DAY: DESTINATION: PACKED: ☐

DAY: EVENING:

ACTIVITY:

OUTFIT:

SHOES:

ACC:

DAY: DESTINATION: PACKED: ☐

DAY: EVENING:

ACTIVITY:

OUTFIT:

SHOES:

ACC:

TRAVEL *Planner*

DATE: **DAY:**

NOTES

6
7
8
9
10
11
12
1
2
3
4
5
6
7
8
9
10
11
12

REMINDERS

TRAVEL EXPENSE *Tracker*

DESTINATION: **BUDGET GOAL:**

DATE:	DESCRIPTION:	CURRENCY:	AMOUNT:

TOTAL EXPENSES:

TRAVEL *Planner*

DESTINATION:

DATES:

BUDGET:

WEATHER:

CURRENCY EXCHANGE:

ACCOMODATION OVERVIEW

NAME: | **LOCATION:** | **DATE:** | **ADDRESS:**

NOTES & TRAVEL DETAILS

TRAVEL *Organizer*

DATE: LOCATION:

DATE: LOCATION:

DAY TRAVEL *Planner*

DATE:	ATTRACTION:	THINGS TO SEE

DATE:	ATTRACTION:	THINGS TO SEE

DAILY TRAVEL *Planner*

DAILY ITINERARY

DATE: _____

LOCATION: _____

BUDGET: _____

TOP ACTIVITIES

MEAL PLANNER

TIME: SCHEDULE:

EXPENSES

TOTAL COST: _____

NOTES:

TRAVEL *Itinerary*

DESTINATION:　　　　　**DATE:**

MON

TUE

WED

THU

FRI

SAT

SUN

DAILY TRAVEL *Planner*

MON

TUE

WED

THU

DAILY TRAVEL *Planner*

FRI

SAT

SUN

TRAVEL *Journal*

TRAVEL *Planner*
PRE-TRAVEL CHECKLIST

1 MONTH BEFORE

- [ ]
- [ ]
- [ ]
- [ ]
- [ ]

2 WEEKS BEFORE

- [ ]
- [ ]
- [ ]
- [ ]
- [ ]

1 WEEK BEFORE

- [ ]
- [ ]
- [ ]
- [ ]
- [ ]

2 DAYS BEFORE

- [ ]
- [ ]
- [ ]
- [ ]
- [ ]

24 HOURS BEFORE

- [ ]
- [ ]
- [ ]
- [ ]
- [ ]

DAY OF TRAVEL

- [ ]
- [ ]
- [ ]
- [ ]
- [ ]

VACATION *Planner*

DAILY ITINERARY

DATE: _____

LOCATION: _____

BUDGET: _____

TOP ACTIVITIES

MEAL PLANNER

TIME: SCHEDULE:

EXPENSES

TOTAL COST: _____

NOTES:

PACKING Check List

DOCUMENTS

- [ ] PASSPORT
- [ ] DRIVER'S LICENSE
- [ ] VISA
- [ ] PLANE TICKETS
- [ ] LOCAL CURRENCY
- [ ] INSURANCE CARD
- [ ] HEALTH CARD
- [ ] OTHER ID
- [ ] HOTEL INFO
- [ ] _____

CLOTHING

- [ ] SOCKS
- [ ] SWIM WEAR
- [ ] T-SHIRTS
- [ ] JEANS/PANTS
- [ ] SHORTS
- [ ] SKIRTS / DRESSES
- [ ] JACKET / COAT
- [ ] SLEEPWEAR
- [ ] SHOES
- [ ] _____

PERSONAL ITEMS

- [ ] SHAMPOO
- [ ] RAZORS
- [ ] COSMETICS
- [ ] HAIR BRUSH
- [ ] LIP BALM
- [ ] WATER BOTTLE
- [ ] SOAP
- [ ] TOOTHBRUSH
- [ ] JEWELRY
- [ ] _____

ELECTRONICS

- [ ] CELL PHONE
- [ ] CHARGER
- [ ] LAPTOP
- [ ] BATTERIES
- [ ] EARPHONES
- [ ] FLASH DRIVE
- [ ] MEMORY CARD
- [ ] _____
- [ ] _____
- [ ] _____

HEALTH & SAFETY

- [ ] HAND SANITIZER
- [ ] SUNSCREEN
- [ ] VITAMIN
- [ ] BANDAIDS
- [ ] ADVIL/TYLENOL
- [ ] GLASSES
- [ ] COLD/FLU MEDS
- [ ] _____
- [ ] _____
- [ ] _____

ESSENTIALS

- [ ] _____
- [ ] _____
- [ ] _____
- [ ] _____
- [ ] _____
- [ ] _____
- [ ] _____
- [ ] _____
- [ ] _____
- [ ] _____

FLIGHT *Information*

DATE: DESTINATION:

AIRLINE:	
BOOKING NUMBER:	
DEPARTURE DATE:	
BOARDING TIME:	
GATE NUMBER:	
SEAT NUMBER:	
FLIGHT DURATION:	
ARRIVAL / LANDING TIME:	

DATE: DESTINATION:

AIRLINE:	
BOOKING NUMBER:	
DEPARTURE DATE:	
BOARDING TIME:	
GATE NUMBER:	
SEAT NUMBER:	
FLIGHT DURATION:	
ARRIVAL / LANDING TIME:	

TRAVEL *Information*

DESTINATION: **DATE:**

PLACES TO STAY

THINGS TO SEE

WHERE TO EAT

RECOMMENDATIONS

TRIP BUDGET *Planner*

TRIP DETAILS:

AMOUNT NEEDED:

OUR GOAL DATE:

DEPOSIT TRACKER

AMOUNT DEPOSITED: **DATE DEPOSITED:**

TRAVEL *Information*

CAR RENTAL INFORMATION

COMPANY:

ADDRESS:

PHONE NUMBER:

CONFIRMATION #:

TOTAL COST:

EVENT INFORMATION

EVENT NAME:

LOCATION:

PHONE NUMBER:

START TIME:

OTHER:

NOTES

TRAVEL *Information*

HOTEL INFORMATION

NAME OF HOTEL:

ADDRESS:

PHONE NUMBER:

CONFIRMATION #:

RATE PER NIGHT:

FLIGHT INFORMATION

AIRLINE:

LOCATION:

FLIGHT #:

CHECK IN TIME:

DEPARTURE TIME:

REFERENCE #:

NOTES

TRIP TO DO List

PACKING *Check List*

DATE OF TRIP: **DURATION:**

OUTFIT *Planner*

DAY:	DESTINATION:	PACKED: ☐

DAY: **EVENING:**

- ACTIVITY:
- OUTFIT:
- SHOES:
- ACC:

DAY:	DESTINATION:	PACKED: ☐

DAY: **EVENING:**

- ACTIVITY:
- OUTFIT:
- SHOES:
- ACC:

DAY:	DESTINATION:	PACKED: ☐

DAY: **EVENING:**

- ACTIVITY:
- OUTFIT:
- SHOES:
- ACC:

OUTFIT *Planner*

DAY: **DESTINATION:** **PACKED:** ☐

DAY: **EVENING:**

ACTIVITY:

OUTFIT:

SHOES:

ACC:

DAY: **DESTINATION:** **PACKED:** ☐

DAY: **EVENING:**

ACTIVITY:

OUTFIT:

SHOES:

ACC:

DAY: **DESTINATION:** **PACKED:** ☐

DAY: **EVENING:**

ACTIVITY:

OUTFIT:

SHOES:

ACC:

OUTFIT *Planner*

DAY: **DESTINATION:**   **PACKED:**

DAY: **EVENING:**

ACTIVITY:

OUTFIT:

SHOES:

ACC:

DAY: **DESTINATION:**   **PACKED:**

DAY: **EVENING:**

ACTIVITY:

OUTFIT:

SHOES:

ACC:

DAY: **DESTINATION:**   **PACKED:**

DAY: **EVENING:**

ACTIVITY:

OUTFIT:

SHOES:

ACC:

OUTFIT *Planner*

| DAY: | DESTINATION: | PACKED: ☐ |

DAY:

ACTIVITY:

OUTFIT:

SHOES:

ACC:

EVENING:

| DAY: | DESTINATION: | PACKED: ☐ |

DAY:

ACTIVITY:

OUTFIT:

SHOES:

ACC:

EVENING:

| DAY: | DESTINATION: | PACKED: ☐ |

DAY:

ACTIVITY:

OUTFIT:

SHOES:

ACC:

EVENING:

OUTFIT *Planner*

DAY: **DESTINATION:**   **PACKED:** ☐

DAY: **EVENING:**

- **ACTIVITY:**
- **OUTFIT:**
- **SHOES:**
- **ACC:**

DAY: **DESTINATION:**   **PACKED:** ☐

DAY: **EVENING:**

- **ACTIVITY:**
- **OUTFIT:**
- **SHOES:**
- **ACC:**

DAY: **DESTINATION:**   **PACKED:** ☐

DAY: **EVENING:**

- **ACTIVITY:**
- **OUTFIT:**
- **SHOES:**
- **ACC:**

OUTFIT *Planner*

| DAY: | DESTINATION: | PACKED: ☐ |

DAY: EVENING:

ACTIVITY:
OUTFIT:
SHOES:
ACC:

| DAY: | DESTINATION: | PACKED: ☐ |

DAY: EVENING:

ACTIVITY:
OUTFIT:
SHOES:
ACC:

| DAY: | DESTINATION: | PACKED: ☐ |

DAY: EVENING:

ACTIVITY:
OUTFIT:
SHOES:
ACC:

TRAVEL *Planner*

DATE: **DAY:**

☀️ ⛅ 🌦️ ☁️ ⛈️

6
7
8
9
10
11
12
1
2
3
4
5
6
7
8
9
10
11
12

NOTES

REMINDERS

TRAVEL EXPENSE *Tracker*

DESTINATION: **BUDGET GOAL:**

DATE:	DESCRIPTION:	CURRENCY:	AMOUNT:

TOTAL EXPENSES:

TRAVEL *Planner*

DESTINATION:

DATES:

BUDGET:

WEATHER:

CURRENCY EXCHANGE:

ACCOMODATION OVERVIEW

NAME:	LOCATION:	DATE:	ADDRESS:

NOTES & TRAVEL DETAILS

TRAVEL *Organizer*

DATE: LOCATION:

DATE: LOCATION:

DAY TRAVEL *Planner*

DATE:	ATTRACTION:	THINGS TO SEE

DATE:	ATTRACTION:	THINGS TO SEE

DAILY TRAVEL *Planner*

DAILY ITINERARY

DATE: _____

LOCATION: _____

BUDGET: _____

TOP ACTIVITIES

MEAL PLANNER

TIME: SCHEDULE:

EXPENSES

TOTAL COST: _____

NOTES:

TRAVEL *Itinerary*

DESTINATION: **DATE:**

MON

TUE

WED

THU

FRI

SAT

SUN

DAILY TRAVEL *Planner*

MON

TUE

WED

THU

DAILY TRAVEL *Planner*

FRI

SAT

SUN

never STOP exploring

TRAVEL *Journal*

TRAVEL *Planner*

PRE-TRAVEL CHECKLIST

1 MONTH BEFORE

- [ ]
- [ ]
- [ ]
- [ ]
- [ ]

2 WEEKS BEFORE

- [ ]
- [ ]
- [ ]
- [ ]
- [ ]

1 WEEK BEFORE

- [ ]
- [ ]
- [ ]
- [ ]
- [ ]

2 DAYS BEFORE

- [ ]
- [ ]
- [ ]
- [ ]
- [ ]

24 HOURS BEFORE

- [ ]
- [ ]
- [ ]
- [ ]
- [ ]

DAY OF TRAVEL

- [ ]
- [ ]
- [ ]
- [ ]
- [ ]

VACATION *Planner*

DAILY ITINERARY

DATE: _____

LOCATION: _____

BUDGET: _____

TOP ACTIVITIES

MEAL PLANNER

TIME: SCHEDULE:

EXPENSES

TOTAL COST: _____

NOTES:

PACKING Check List

DOCUMENTS

- ☐ PASSPORT
- ☐ DRIVER'S LICENSE
- ☐ VISA
- ☐ PLANE TICKETS
- ☐ LOCAL CURRENCY
- ☐ INSURANCE CARD
- ☐ HEALTH CARD
- ☐ OTHER ID
- ☐ HOTEL INFO
- ☐ _____

CLOTHING

- ☐ SOCKS
- ☐ SWIM WEAR
- ☐ T-SHIRTS
- ☐ JEANS/PANTS
- ☐ SHORTS
- ☐ SKIRTS / DRESSES
- ☐ JACKET / COAT
- ☐ SLEEPWEAR
- ☐ SHOES
- ☐ _____

PERSONAL ITEMS

- ☐ SHAMPOO
- ☐ RAZORS
- ☐ COSMETICS
- ☐ HAIR BRUSH
- ☐ LIP BALM
- ☐ WATER BOTTLE
- ☐ SOAP
- ☐ TOOTHBRUSH
- ☐ JEWELRY
- ☐ _____

ELECTRONICS

- ☐ CELL PHONE
- ☐ CHARGER
- ☐ LAPTOP
- ☐ BATTERIES
- ☐ EARPHONES
- ☐ FLASH DRIVE
- ☐ MEMORY CARD
- ☐ _____
- ☐ _____
- ☐ _____

HEALTH & SAFETY

- ☐ HAND SANITIZER
- ☐ SUNSCREEN
- ☐ VITAMIN
- ☐ BANDAIDS
- ☐ ADVIL/TYLENOL
- ☐ GLASSES
- ☐ COLD/FLU MEDS
- ☐ _____
- ☐ _____
- ☐ _____

ESSENTIALS

- ☐ _____
- ☐ _____
- ☐ _____
- ☐ _____
- ☐ _____
- ☐ _____
- ☐ _____
- ☐ _____
- ☐ _____
- ☐ _____

FLIGHT *Information*

DATE: DESTINATION:

AIRLINE:	
BOOKING NUMBER:	
DEPARTURE DATE:	
BOARDING TIME:	
GATE NUMBER:	
SEAT NUMBER:	
FLIGHT DURATION:	
ARRIVAL / LANDING TIME:	

DATE: DESTINATION:

AIRLINE:	
BOOKING NUMBER:	
DEPARTURE DATE:	
BOARDING TIME:	
GATE NUMBER:	
SEAT NUMBER:	
FLIGHT DURATION:	
ARRIVAL / LANDING TIME:	

TRAVEL *Information*

DESTINATION: **DATE:**

PLACES TO STAY

THINGS TO SEE

WHERE TO EAT

RECOMMENDATIONS

TRIP BUDGET *Planner*

TRIP DETAILS:

AMOUNT NEEDED:

OUR GOAL DATE:

DEPOSIT TRACKER

AMOUNT DEPOSITED: **DATE DEPOSITED:**

TRAVEL *Information*

CAR RENTAL INFORMATION

COMPANY:

ADDRESS:

PHONE NUMBER:

CONFIRMATION #:

TOTAL COST:

EVENT INFORMATION

EVENT NAME:

LOCATION:

PHONE NUMBER:

START TIME:

OTHER:

NOTES

TRAVEL *Information*

HOTEL INFORMATION

NAME OF HOTEL:

ADDRESS:

PHONE NUMBER:

CONFIRMATION #:

RATE PER NIGHT:

FLIGHT INFORMATION

AIRLINE:

LOCATION:

FLIGHT #:

CHECK IN TIME:

DEPARTURE TIME:

REFERENCE #:

NOTES

TRIP TO DO *List*

PACKING *Check List*

DATE OF TRIP: _____ **DURATION:** _____

OUTFIT *Planner*

DAY: **DESTINATION:** **PACKED:** ☐

DAY: **EVENING:**

ACTIVITY:

OUTFIT:

SHOES:

ACC:

DAY: **DESTINATION:** **PACKED:** ☐

DAY: **EVENING:**

ACTIVITY:

OUTFIT:

SHOES:

ACC:

DAY: **DESTINATION:** **PACKED:** ☐

DAY: **EVENING:**

ACTIVITY:

OUTFIT:

SHOES:

ACC:

OUTFIT *Planner*

DAY: **DESTINATION:** **PACKED:** ☐

DAY: **EVENING:**

- ACTIVITY:
- OUTFIT:
- SHOES:
- ACC:

DAY: **DESTINATION:** **PACKED:** ☐

DAY: **EVENING:**

- ACTIVITY:
- OUTFIT:
- SHOES:
- ACC:

DAY: **DESTINATION:** **PACKED:** ☐

DAY: **EVENING:**

- ACTIVITY:
- OUTFIT:
- SHOES:
- ACC:

OUTFIT *Planner*

| DAY: | DESTINATION: | PACKED: ☐ |

DAY: EVENING:

ACTIVITY:

OUTFIT:

SHOES:

ACC:

| DAY: | DESTINATION: | PACKED: ☐ |

DAY: EVENING:

ACTIVITY:

OUTFIT:

SHOES:

ACC:

| DAY: | DESTINATION: | PACKED: ☐ |

DAY: EVENING:

ACTIVITY:

OUTFIT:

SHOES:

ACC:

OUTFIT Planner

| DAY: | DESTINATION: | PACKED: |

DAY: EVENING:

ACTIVITY:
OUTFIT:
SHOES:
ACC:

| DAY: | DESTINATION: | PACKED: |

DAY: EVENING:

ACTIVITY:
OUTFIT:
SHOES:
ACC:

| DAY: | DESTINATION: | PACKED: |

DAY: EVENING:

ACTIVITY:
OUTFIT:
SHOES:
ACC:

OUTFIT *Planner*

DAY: **DESTINATION:**   **PACKED:** ☐

DAY: **EVENING:**

- **ACTIVITY:**
- **OUTFIT:**
- **SHOES:**
- **ACC:**

DAY: **DESTINATION:**   **PACKED:** ☐

DAY: **EVENING:**

- **ACTIVITY:**
- **OUTFIT:**
- **SHOES:**
- **ACC:**

DAY: **DESTINATION:**   **PACKED:** ☐

DAY: **EVENING:**

- **ACTIVITY:**
- **OUTFIT:**
- **SHOES:**
- **ACC:**

OUTFIT *Planner*

DAY:	DESTINATION:	PACKED: ☐

DAY: | **EVENING:**

ACTIVITY:
OUTFIT:
SHOES:
ACC:

DAY:	DESTINATION:	PACKED: ☐

DAY: | **EVENING:**

ACTIVITY:
OUTFIT:
SHOES:
ACC:

DAY:	DESTINATION:	PACKED: ☐

DAY: | **EVENING:**

ACTIVITY:
OUTFIT:
SHOES:
ACC:

TRAVEL *Planner*

DATE: **DAY:**

☀️ ⛅ 🌦️ ☁️ ⛈️

6
7
8
9
10
11
12
1
2
3
4
5
6
7
8
9
10
11
12

NOTES

REMINDERS

TRAVEL EXPENSE *Tracker*

DESTINATION: **BUDGET GOAL:**

DATE:	DESCRIPTION:	CURRENCY:	AMOUNT:

TOTAL EXPENSES:

TRAVEL *Planner*

DESTINATION:

DATES:

BUDGET:

WEATHER:

CURRENCY EXCHANGE:

ACCOMODATION OVERVIEW

NAME:	LOCATION:	DATE:	ADDRESS:

NOTES & TRAVEL DETAILS

TRAVEL *Organizer*

DATE: LOCATION:

DATE: LOCATION:

DAY TRAVEL *Planner*

DATE:	ATTRACTION:	THINGS TO SEE

DATE:	ATTRACTION:	THINGS TO SEE

DAILY TRAVEL *Planner*

DAILY ITINERARY

DATE: _____

LOCATION: _____

BUDGET: _____

☀️ ⛅ 🌦️ ☁️ ⛈️

TOP ACTIVITIES

MEAL PLANNER

TIME: **SCHEDULE:**

EXPENSES

TOTAL COST: _____

NOTES:

TRAVEL *Itinerary*

DESTINATION: **DATE:**

MON

TUE

WED

THU

FRI

SAT

SUN

DAILY TRAVEL *Planner*

MON

TUE

WED

THU

DAILY TRAVEL *Planner*

FRI

SAT

SUN

never STOP exploring

TRAVEL *Journal*

TRAVEL *Planner*

PRE-TRAVEL CHECKLIST

1 MONTH BEFORE

- [ ]
- [ ]
- [ ]
- [ ]
- [ ]

2 WEEKS BEFORE

- [ ]
- [ ]
- [ ]
- [ ]
- [ ]

1 WEEK BEFORE

- [ ]
- [ ]
- [ ]
- [ ]
- [ ]

2 DAYS BEFORE

- [ ]
- [ ]
- [ ]
- [ ]
- [ ]

24 HOURS BEFORE

- [ ]
- [ ]
- [ ]
- [ ]
- [ ]

DAY OF TRAVEL

- [ ]
- [ ]
- [ ]
- [ ]
- [ ]

VACATION *Planner*

DAILY ITINERARY

DATE: _____

LOCATION: _____

BUDGET: _____

☀️ ⛅ 🌦️ ☁️ ⛈️

TOP ACTIVITIES

MEAL PLANNER

TIME: SCHEDULE:

EXPENSES

TOTAL COST: _____

NOTES:

PACKING Check List

DOCUMENTS

- [ ] PASSPORT
- [ ] DRIVER'S LICENSE
- [ ] VISA
- [ ] PLANE TICKETS
- [ ] LOCAL CURRENCY
- [ ] INSURANCE CARD
- [ ] HEALTH CARD
- [ ] OTHER ID
- [ ] HOTEL INFO
- [ ] _____

CLOTHING

- [ ] SOCKS
- [ ] SWIM WEAR
- [ ] T-SHIRTS
- [ ] JEANS/PANTS
- [ ] SHORTS
- [ ] SKIRTS / DRESSES
- [ ] JACKET / COAT
- [ ] SLEEPWEAR
- [ ] SHOES
- [ ] _____

PERSONAL ITEMS

- [ ] SHAMPOO
- [ ] RAZORS
- [ ] COSMETICS
- [ ] HAIR BRUSH
- [ ] LIP BALM
- [ ] WATER BOTTLE
- [ ] SOAP
- [ ] TOOTHBRUSH
- [ ] JEWELRY
- [ ] _____

ELECTRONICS

- [ ] CELL PHONE
- [ ] CHARGER
- [ ] LAPTOP
- [ ] BATTERIES
- [ ] EARPHONES
- [ ] FLASH DRIVE
- [ ] MEMORY CARD
- [ ] _____
- [ ] _____
- [ ] _____

HEALTH & SAFETY

- [ ] HAND SANITIZER
- [ ] SUNSCREEN
- [ ] VITAMIN
- [ ] BANDAIDS
- [ ] ADVIL/TYLENOL
- [ ] GLASSES
- [ ] COLD/FLU MEDS
- [ ] _____
- [ ] _____
- [ ] _____

ESSENTIALS

- [ ] _____
- [ ] _____
- [ ] _____
- [ ] _____
- [ ] _____
- [ ] _____
- [ ] _____
- [ ] _____
- [ ] _____
- [ ] _____

FLIGHT *Information*

DATE: DESTINATION:

AIRLINE:	
BOOKING NUMBER:	
DEPARTURE DATE:	
BOARDING TIME:	
GATE NUMBER:	
SEAT NUMBER:	
FLIGHT DURATION:	
ARRIVAL / LANDING TIME:	

DATE: DESTINATION:

AIRLINE:	
BOOKING NUMBER:	
DEPARTURE DATE:	
BOARDING TIME:	
GATE NUMBER:	
SEAT NUMBER:	
FLIGHT DURATION:	
ARRIVAL / LANDING TIME:	

TRAVEL *Information*

DESTINATION: **DATE:**

PLACES TO STAY

THINGS TO SEE

WHERE TO EAT

RECOMMENDATIONS

TRIP BUDGET *Planner*

TRIP DETAILS:

AMOUNT NEEDED:

OUR GOAL DATE:

DEPOSIT TRACKER

AMOUNT DEPOSITED:　　　　　　　**DATE DEPOSITED:**

TRAVEL *Information*

CAR RENTAL INFORMATION

COMPANY:

ADDRESS:

PHONE NUMBER:

CONFIRMATION #:

TOTAL COST:

EVENT INFORMATION

EVENT NAME:

LOCATION:

PHONE NUMBER:

START TIME:

OTHER:

NOTES

TRAVEL *Information*

HOTEL INFORMATION

NAME OF HOTEL:

ADDRESS:

PHONE NUMBER:

CONFIRMATION #:

RATE PER NIGHT:

FLIGHT INFORMATION

AIRLINE:

LOCATION:

FLIGHT #:

CHECK IN TIME:

DEPARTURE TIME:

REFERENCE #:

NOTES

TRIP TO DO List

PACKING *Check List*

DATE OF TRIP: **DURATION:**

OUTFIT *Planner*

DAY: **DESTINATION:** **PACKED:** ☐

DAY: **EVENING:**

ACTIVITY:
OUTFIT:
SHOES:
ACC:

DAY: **DESTINATION:** **PACKED:** ☐

DAY: **EVENING:**

ACTIVITY:
OUTFIT:
SHOES:
ACC:

DAY: **DESTINATION:** **PACKED:** ☐

DAY: **EVENING:**

ACTIVITY:
OUTFIT:
SHOES:
ACC:

OUTFIT *Planner*

DAY: **DESTINATION:** **PACKED:** ☐

DAY: **EVENING:**

ACTIVITY:

OUTFIT:

SHOES:

ACC:

DAY: **DESTINATION:** **PACKED:** ☐

DAY: **EVENING:**

ACTIVITY:

OUTFIT:

SHOES:

ACC:

DAY: **DESTINATION:** **PACKED:** ☐

DAY: **EVENING:**

ACTIVITY:

OUTFIT:

SHOES:

ACC:

OUTFIT *Planner*

DAY: **DESTINATION:**   **PACKED:** ☐

DAY: **EVENING:**

ACTIVITY:

OUTFIT:

SHOES:

ACC:

DAY: **DESTINATION:**   **PACKED:** ☐

DAY: **EVENING:**

ACTIVITY:

OUTFIT:

SHOES:

ACC:

DAY: **DESTINATION:**   **PACKED:** ☐

DAY: **EVENING:**

ACTIVITY:

OUTFIT:

SHOES:

ACC:

OUTFIT *Planner*

DAY: **DESTINATION:** **PACKED:** ☐

DAY: **EVENING:**

ACTIVITY:

OUTFIT:

SHOES:

ACC:

DAY: **DESTINATION:** **PACKED:** ☐

DAY: **EVENING:**

ACTIVITY:

OUTFIT:

SHOES:

ACC:

DAY: **DESTINATION:** **PACKED:** ☐

DAY: **EVENING:**

ACTIVITY:

OUTFIT:

SHOES:

ACC:

OUTFIT *Planner*

DAY: **DESTINATION:** **PACKED:** ☐

DAY:	EVENING:
ACTIVITY:	
OUTFIT:	
SHOES:	
ACC:	

DAY: **DESTINATION:** **PACKED:** ☐

DAY:	EVENING:
ACTIVITY:	
OUTFIT:	
SHOES:	
ACC:	

DAY: **DESTINATION:** **PACKED:** ☐

DAY:	EVENING:
ACTIVITY:	
OUTFIT:	
SHOES:	
ACC:	

OUTFIT *Planner*

| DAY: | DESTINATION: | PACKED: ☐ |

DAY:

ACTIVITY:

OUTFIT:

SHOES:

ACC:

EVENING:

| DAY: | DESTINATION: | PACKED: ☐ |

DAY:

ACTIVITY:

OUTFIT:

SHOES:

ACC:

EVENING:

| DAY: | DESTINATION: | PACKED: ☐ |

DAY:

ACTIVITY:

OUTFIT:

SHOES:

ACC:

EVENING:

TRAVEL Planner

DATE:

DAY:

NOTES

REMINDERS

Time	
6	
7	
8	
9	
10	
11	
12	
1	
2	
3	
4	
5	
6	
7	
8	
9	
10	
11	
12	

TRAVEL EXPENSE *Tracker*

DESTINATION: BUDGET GOAL:

DATE:	DESCRIPTION:	CURRENCY:	AMOUNT:

TOTAL EXPENSES:

TRAVEL *Planner*

DESTINATION:

DATES:

BUDGET:

WEATHER:

CURRENCY EXCHANGE:

ACCOMODATION OVERVIEW

NAME:	LOCATION:	DATE:	ADDRESS:

NOTES & TRAVEL DETAILS

TRAVEL *Organizer*

DATE: **LOCATION:**

DATE: **LOCATION:**

DAY TRAVEL *Planner*

DATE:	ATTRACTION:	THINGS TO SEE

DATE:	ATTRACTION:	THINGS TO SEE

DAILY TRAVEL *Planner*

DAILY ITINERARY

DATE: _____

LOCATION: _____

BUDGET: _____

TOP ACTIVITIES

MEAL PLANNER

TIME: SCHEDULE:

EXPENSES

TOTAL COST: _____

NOTES:

TRAVEL *Itinerary*

DESTINATION: **DATE:**

MON

TUE

WED

THU

FRI

SAT

SUN

DAILY TRAVEL *Planner*

MON

TUE

WED

THU

DAILY TRAVEL *Planner*

FRI

SAT

SUN

never STOP exploring

TRAVEL *Journal*

Made in the USA
Coppell, TX
04 June 2022